Carla Whittier

Stay with me

Keeping your relationship

@Carla Whittier 2022

Table of content

INTRODUCTION

Beginning a relationship is dependably fun and invigorating, however making a relationship last is difficult work. Whenever you've gotten comfortable your relationship, you need to keep a fair progression of correspondence and to keep on valuing your experience with your cherished one. Making a relationship last isn't generally fun, however the advantages of keeping a long haul and serious relationship far offset the troubles that you might confront. If you have any desire to know how to make your relationship last, simply follow these tips.

CHAPTER 1

Knowing if you are ready for relationship

Being prepared for a satisfying relationship is not the same as needing to be in one. At the point when you're genuinely prepared, it implies you're ready to give love in a solid manner (and you're prepared to get it, as well!). Before you make a plunge, look at our pre-relationship agenda beneath:

You understand what you need from a relationship. Long haul or present moment, serious or relaxed, open or shut — it's down to you to conclude what you need and to convey that to your accomplice.

You've contemplated your necessities, limits, and big issues. You would rather not become involved with a relationship that doesn't serve your bliss. Think about what you can and can't acknowledge before you engage with somebody. Could you remain with a faithless accomplice? Might you at any point deal with a too bustling accomplice to hang out routinely?

You comprehend your relationship examples and you're chipping away at them. Do you have a restless connection style? Perhaps you're dealing with giving accomplices more autonomy. Or then again, do you have an avoidant connection style? All things considered, your center may be correspondence.

You have sensible assumptions for your relationship. You realize that connections require adaptability and acknowledgment. Things won't generally be great, however you're focused on figuring out through your problems.

You realize that genuine, aware openness is of the utmost importance. During contentions, your objective will be to track down an answer, not to win or to control your accomplice. You're prepared to utilize "I feel" proclamations and to assume liability when you commit errors.

You'll be a trustworthy and steady accomplice. In great times and in terrible, you anticipate being there for them (very much like you'd anticipate that your accomplice should accomplish for you!). You need to be somebody your accomplice can depend on — and that implies showing up when it counts.

You intend to certify and regard your accomplice. You realize that solid connections are about sure communications. You know that praising, saying thanks to, and offering grace to your accomplice will be critical.

You comprehend that in a relationship, you ought to both have your own personalities. You know that for you two to be genuinely content, you'll need to carry on with your own lives, as well. The interests and individuals that are essential to you presently ought to in any case mean quite a bit to you in a relationship.

You intend to keep dealing with yourself while in a relationship. By the day's end, you know that you'll both should be glad for the relationship to work out. You anticipate focusing on your mind-sets, rehearsing taking care of oneself, and doing what fulfills you — even while you support your accomplice, as well.

Chapter 2

Relationship happiness

Bliss inside a relationship is difficult to characterize. Not exclusively is every relationship unique, yet inside every relationship, every individual characterizes bliss during a singular way. Certain individuals view satisfaction as a serene struggle free life. For some's purposes, bliss includes an unlimited measure of tomfoolery, extraordinary closeness or bunches of chuckling. Anything that your definition, it straightforwardly connects to your assumptions, wants, needs and wishes — and those things can change after some time.

What holds consistent are 7 explicit ways of behaving and credits opened up underneath that, in my experience, can nearly make sure the probability of long haul achievement and satisfaction in a relationship.

On the off chance that you simply make progress toward coordinating these keys into your regular routine, you'll definitely encounter more noteworthy euphoria and less struggle in your essential connections.

1. Regard

Each fruitful relationship is predicated on an underpinning of regard. Regard implies thinking often about your accomplice's needs and wishes and continuously considering them prior to talking or acting. the idea is that your accomplice will keep similar rules. My authority definition is as per the following: Respect implies putting the solace, prosperity and bliss of the individual you're with at the same level to your own.

2. Dependability

We feel cheerful once we realize that somebody has us covered. Connections have the simplest achievement when each accomplice centers around supporting each other consistently. This truly intends that assuming somebody is offending your accomplice, you'll either back your accomplice up straightforwardly or support the person in question from in the background. This additionally intends that assuming your accomplice has accomplished something you accept is off-base or that you simply don't endorse, that you simply address the person in question secretly about the issue, never before others.

3. Need

To fabricate a more grounded positive relationship, let your accomplice in thereon the person is fundamentally important. Commit investment to talking and tending to at least one another's needs and needs. be sure that you two have "quality time" alone to associate and appreciate each other's conversation. Despite the very fact that work, youngsters and different commitments are additionally needs, find the equilibrium so your association isn't disregarde

4. PICK YOUR BATTLES

Solid and cheerful couples know while to boost issues and when to set them to the side. My guideline: If you'll let something go, continue on regardless partake in your accomplice ... let it go! within the event that you can't continue on and are ruminating or agonizing over something, then, at that time , bring it up. At the purpose when you truly do bring it up, ensure it's in a quiet way, privately and at a great time for both of you to examine it. Never bring something disturbing up in bed, and never in earshot of youngsters or other family or companions.

5. Cherishing GESTURES

The idea "Talk is cheap" is a significant one with regards to connections. it is not sufficient to just feel that you love somebody, you ought to likewise show that you love that individual. Utilize kind words, be genuinely friendly, begin from little love notes around the house ... whether it's a verbal motion or a material one, make sure that you are

telling your accomplice plainly that you love the person in question.

6. Set forth THE Energy

Accomplices during a fruitful relationship comprehend that you really want to invest the effort to keep things moving along as planned. that suggests in some cases you really want to would things that you truly do like to do on the grounds that it is important to your accomplice. Different times it implies you would like to invest that additional energy to quiet down or hear out your accomplice's interests, no matter whether that isn't the least demanding or most helpful thing to do at the time. Connections take an excellent deal of work in the event that they will be blissful, effective and sturdy .

Chapter 3

Understanding

Understanding connections is hard! Two singularities together, unfeignedly related, and attempting to investigate greater part coming to one another is tangled. It gets boundlessly further persistently if there's a shortfall of understanding between those two singularities.

Seeing each other in a relationship gives off an impression of being starting sufficient on a shallow position, actually executing great can challenge. I hear visitors continually grieve that they don't feel appreciated or fight to sort out their abettor .

All by every, how might we foster a relationship of getting a handle on between two individuals? How should we upscale sort out somebody in an unexpected way? What does being understanding seeing somebody feel to be?

peruse on to sort out some way to be genuinely understanding in a relationship and how to get reputation to get a handle on you, too.

What is the importance then to get it?

it is ordinary yet likewise puzzled to arrange grasping associations. Having understanding associations doesn't mean you agree, as, or have to oblige what someone else is referring to or feeling.

In understanding associations, you can connect with the approaching existent, represent them to assume and feel the way that they do, and respect that what they are experiencing is about them and not about you.

Why is sorting out critical in a relationship?

Regardless, you might be asking yourself," why is it crucial to see each other?" In case we watch around one another, appreciate each other's conversation, and celebrate the good life, why help we've to raise out hell to create getting a handle on associations, too?

The meaning of understanding in associations goes quite far past the face and is the best approach to opening a lot of other critical bits of an exceptional relationship.

Two expressions of remorse for why understanding is critical seeing somebody affiliation and trust.

Exactly when an abettor feels like we're showing up with both love and understanding, they feel really seen and heard. These are two of the most widely respected impacts I hear my visitors share that they need to feel specific and related with their life mate.

Bit by bit guidelines to additionally foster relationship understanding

Significant Couple At Home Showing Love Each Other On Coffee Table

1. Demand what you want

If you are feeling misgauged in your relationship, you should get what you really want. An uncommon spot to start is telling your abettor ," What I need from you is understanding."

Anyway, don't stop there.

Get a handle on what you mean by" understanding" and what you acknowledge it looks like to act in a seeing way can help your join with giving you what you want.

Your abettor could have a substitute investigation of what it infers and looks like to be understanding, so by partaking what you are looking for, you can assist with promising you get what you really want, and your abettor doesn't have to figure. Win, win!

2. Tune in with interest rather than judgment and don't make it about you

At the point when we differ or feel went after, we will generally get guarded and critical of what our accomplice is imparting to us. This can move us towards a battle, misconstruing our accomplice, and at last difficulties our relationship and private association.

This features why understanding is significant seeing someone.

In the event that we have understanding connections, we don't rush to make judgment calls as frequently, and we can become inquisitive about the thing our accomplice is sharing rather than cautious.

Take a stab at standing by listening to your accomplice like they're recounting another person (regardless of whether it's about you.) Get inquisitive about how they're feeling here, why they figure the manner in which they do, and what influence this has on them. Attempt to pull together your consideration on them and their story rather than how you may be feeling about what they're talking about.

Ask strong, inquisitive inquiries to urge your accomplice to share more about the thing they're thinking, feeling, and encountering so you can extend how you might interpret them.

Oppose your desire to respond or retaliate. You can't tune in for understanding in the event that contemplating you will say straightaway!

3. Practice sympathy

Compassion is a particularly vital expertise and is key for grasping in a relationship.

Sympathy permits us to take point of view on what somebody is talking about, envision how or why they may be feeling as such without feeling the feeling ourselves.

For instance, assuming that your accomplice is sharing they felt decided by something you said, yet you didn't expect to pass judgment on them, compassion can assist you with understanding where they're coming from regardless of whether you conflict. (You don't need to consent to rehearse compassion.)

By connecting with their experience rather than why they're encountering it, you can more readily comprehend and uphold your accomplice.

4. Figure out how to tune in past the words that are being said

The words we say are just a part of our general correspondence. Frequently in correspondence, we get so lost in the words that we neglect to likewise focus on the individual saying those words.

Correspondence goes past the sentences your accomplice is talking resoundingly.

Attempt to focus on your accomplice's all's various angles while they are offering to you.

How is their manner of speaking? Is it safe to say that they are talking quick or slow? How can they hold themselves? Gazing straight toward you or the floor? Is it true or not that they are nervous, breathing rapidly, or stammering?

These prompts can assist you with better comprehension the individual's insight past the words they're utilizing.

Words just get us such a long ways in grasping connections.

The video beneath talks about the training craft of intelligent tuning in. For fruitful and understanding connections, this assists in handy solutions and functions as an extraordinary correspondence with tooling.

5. Attempt to comprehend prior to attempting to be perceived

Whenever we speak with an accomplice, we're frequently attempting to feature our focuses, guarantee we are heard and perceived.

Every individual's occupation to be sure is to go to bat for themselves and offer their considerations and sentiments. Understanding in a relationship is a two-way road, and the two accomplices should be heard. Neither one of you can pay attention to assuming you're too bustling talking and zeroing in on yourself.

Assuming you're attempting to work on grasping in your relationship, check whether you can put your accomplice first and gain understanding before you offer your side.

By accounting for each accomplice to be entirely perceived, you establish the groundwork for more profound association and trust.

On the off chance that you actually have a detached or baffled outlook on your relationship understanding or with your accomplice, you should seriously mull over signing up for an internet based marriage course like this or counseling a specialist or relationship mentor.

Chapter 4

Commitment

While endeavoring to make a cherishing, sound close connection, it is critical to have an exact guide for the excursion. The vast majority of our way of life's guides have underscored dream, deception and refusal, and the people who follow those guides will more often than not have miserable, struggle ridden connections. What follows is a reality-based guide which comes from examination into couples' genuine encounters of being in long haul connections.

While scholars differ on the specific name and number of the stages couples progress through, there is an overall agreement that couples go through some variant of the accompanying stages. Not every person goes through every one of the stages and a few couples might go through them in an alternate grouping, yet for most couples this is the regulating experience in a drawn out serious relationship.

1. Heartfelt LOVE

This is the affection that Hollywood loves to advance as the main sort of adoration. Heartfelt love is magnificent, simple, and easy. It is extremely unconstrained and alive. The sentiments and insights that go through the two individuals are that we are one; we are something similar. You are great. I can give and get love with practically no work required. There is a colossal accentuation on expanding similitudes and limiting contrasts. There is a conviction and assumption that you will give most or every one of my needs, needs, wants. There is by and large a serious level of energy and sentiments and articulations of sentiment come effectively and frequently. The accomplices ponder each other continually, and visually engage and are exceptionally loving when they are together. Many individuals experience this as living in a condition of close steady euphoria and fixation. There is a conviction that these sentiments and encounters will continue everlastingly, that 'we won't ever differ on anything', and that in some way destiny or powers bigger than themselves have united them.

This stage for the most part endures from a half year to two years, and is the SHORTEST phase of any of the phases of long haul serious relationships.

2. Changing in accordance with REALITY

Ok, reality. Definitely, typically, at last, reality raises its (appalling?) head and the air pocket blasts on the Romantic stage. Some of the time it is a sluggish release, different times an unexpected and complete victory. In any case, one way or the other, something happens which causes a minor or significant clash in the new relationship. In some cases the trigger is living respectively and sharing family errands and encountering individual propensities very close. Now and then it is a demonstration of misdirection which is found. Here and there it is arranging a wedding, purchasing a house, or sharing funds. Anything the reason, after the contention happens, it becomes difficult to proceed with the dream that this individual and this relationship are insusceptible from battle, from exertion, from the real world. Contrasts which were recently darkened out of nowhere become apparent. Clashes, nerves, disillusionment and hurt supplant the easy progression of the Romantic stage. There is a feeling that this individual isn't living up your deepest desires, and there is a going with loss of closeness. Continuously every individual is compelled to surrender a portion of their most loved heartfelt dreams, or to grip to them frantically in a condition of disavowal.

In this stage, it is normal to feel as though a person or thing or even Life itself has swindled you or denied you of something valuable, practically like a phase of lamenting the deficiency of something guiltless and great. There is a longing to be close once more yet disarray as how to make that. The initial time fears of closeness start to emerge. Abruptly the couple should figure out how to manage genuine contrasts, how to manage struggle, and how to coordinate being an autonomous individual as well as somebody in a personal connection.

To put it plainly, Adjusting to Reality is the stage where the Real Relationship starts.

3. THE POWER STRUGGLE

As the dissatisfaction of the Adjusting to Reality stage develops, the couple will in general have more conflicts. Minor issues explode into bigger contentions. Hollering shows up interestingly, in the event that it at any point will. The two accomplices dive in their heels and safeguard their situations on issues furiously. Every individual dives in their heels and safeguards their turf. This once-delicate easy cherishing relationship has turned into a milestone and developed into a day to day Power Struggle. This is a run of the mill stage in the improvement of a drawn out serious relationship.

Without precedent for the relationship, there are intermittent or continuous contemplations of leaving the relationship. This individual who as of late seemed, by all accounts, to be the encapsulation of unadulterated love and satisfaction in your eyes abruptly appears to be conceited and not reliable. Questions emerge concerning whether the other individual truly cherishes you. There are reliable sensations of uncertainty and outrage. Accusing and blaming turns into the most well-known structure for collaboration. Each accomplice fears surrendering, and needs the other to change. This is where profound feelings of hatred start to shape, which assuming left unrestrained, become the disease that in the end consumes all the affection and delicacy that has preceded. Mockery and antagonism go into day to day discussions.

This doesn't need to mean the demise of the relationship. The undertakings for the couple here are to foster critical thinking, compromise and arranging abilities. The struggles will plainly not disappear all alone. Every individual much figure out how to listen consciously to their accomplice's situation, regardless of whether they concur with it. They should figure out how to help their accomplice's own development, regardless of whether they feel it undermines their own. They might see the starting points of the examples of their struggles (and their useless approaches to settling them) in their group of beginning.

4. RE-EVALUATION

The Power Struggle is truly and sincerely depleting, and in the event that the couple can make due, they enter the following stage, of a cognizant Re-Evaluation of the association . Though the main responsibility one makes is normally founded on projections of imagination, this Re-Evaluation thinks about the truth and fears and safeguards of every individual. Do I really need to remain with this individual? You know who this individual is currently, you perceive their constraints, and you perceive the scope of which they are equipped for improving or improving. Knowing all that, does one actually need to remain? That is the issue that gets replied during this stage.

The two individuals will generally show outward to determine their issues, as opposed to toward one another. Subsequently, separation anxieties come up unequivocally here. am I ready to make without help from anyone else? Am I truly OK how I am? Will any other person think that I'm alluring or engaging?

The two individuals inwardly (and now and again genuinely) withdraw and pull out during this stage, which makes it the stage during which partition, separate as well as an issue are probably to happen. Sensations of disdain are less extreme during this stage, on the grounds that the effect in the relationship is probably going to be exceptionally level and void. The relationship irregular, best case scenario, and more probable non-existent. Things are ready for an undertaking to burst on the scene, and at times an individual in this stage will start to trust in person of the other gender. This partner will handle increasingly more significance in the individual's life, on account of their poverty and weakness, and that they will frequently get genuinely extremely involved without deliberately acknowledging it. At presently even the smallest friendship resembles tossing a match in the woodland on a warm summer day, and an over the top , extreme issue will start.

The peril is that when an undertaking starts at this stage, it's exceedingly difficult for the relationship to recuperate. the primary relationship has excessively minimal making it work in the method of satisfaction on one or the other side, and thusly the unavoidable correlations between the undertaking and the relationship seem like everything turned inside out.

A detachment are much of the time valuable here to assist every individual with acquiring point of view, due that can likewise prompt the end of the relationship assuming that external delights appear to overshadow the vacancy of the relationship.

The undertaking for each individual here is to remain present and honor their responsibility, grow independently and be prepared to consider their accomplice to be a different individual. this is many times the main way the relationship can make due and move into the following stage.

5. Compromise

In this stage, after the space of the Re-assessment, in the event that the association has made due, there's a resurrection of interest in drawing nearer and interfacing once more. Realizing all that they know, coming from the real world and not dream, there's a choice to have the eagerness to attempt indeed. there's an open acknowledgment of the struggles and contrasts in the relationship, however they're drawn closer with an alternate demeanor: they are utilized as any open doors for finding out around oneself and the other individual. they're impetuses for development and change. there's an acknowledgment that the distinctions are genuine and will not disappear, which neither one individuals can truly change the other. In this way starts a course of battling to make a legit, certifiable personal connection. Once more, individuals associate and consequently the relationship again starts to create continuous fulfillment for the two accomplices.

In this stage there is likewise a more profound feeling of getting a sense of ownership with one's part in struggle and in absence of fulfillment. everybody might perceive the connection between what they realized as kids in their groups of beginning and how they approach close connections. They own their mutilations and projections onto their accomplices. they begin to see their accomplice as they see themselves, as a fairly imperfect yet good one that is putting forth a genuine attempt to cherish and be close nevertheless deal with their own requirements.

There is a more profound acknowledgment in this stage that any relationship can't and won't save you in any sense. you keep on having your own singular requirements and issues and they doesn't disappear in light of the fact that you are seeing someone. However, the a piece of your life that can be sustained and partaken in a cherishing, tolerating relationship is moreover genuine and in this stage every individual looks to the next for that association. The conflict is finished, the struggles are acknowledged, and there's an earnest craving to figure out how to deal with through the problems to a delightful goal.

6. Acknowledgment

The last stage in a serious relationship, which specialists gauge under 5% of couples at any point reach, is one of complete Acceptance. There is a joining of the need of oneself and the requirements of the relationship. Every individual gets a sense of ownership with their own necessities, for their own singular lives, and furthermore for offering help for their accomplice. An elevated degree of warmth is available. The couple can keep a harmony among independence and association. Clashes actually emerge once in a while, yet because of the battles of the past stage, two or three has sorted out some way to determine most contentions moderately rapidly. Feelings of disdain are not many. There are not many astonishments: these are individuals who know each other and know what's in store. They acknowledge what they are getting, with no refusal or dream included. They cooperate collectively to remain associated and furthermore keep up with their own personalities.

These are the six phases that most couples go through during a drawn out serious relationship. While few out of every odd couple goes through each stage or in that careful arrangement, in any case this guide, in light of the examination on genuine couples' encounters of close connection, actually gives the best guide we have accessible for diagramming the most probable way of a drawn out serious relationship. Furthermore, in the event that we have a guide, we can outline the best and least troublesome way to the objective of a satisfying, personal connection.

www.ingramcontent.com/pod-product-compliance
Lightning Source LLC
LaVergne TN
LVHW080557160826
845677LV00010B/1882

* 9 7 9 8 8 4 4 4 2 4 6 9 4 *